FLORIDA
VACATIONLANDS
A PICTURE MEMORY

Text
Bill Harris

Captions
Laura Potts

Design
Teddy Hartshorn

Photo Editor
Annette Lerner

Photography
Colour Library Books Ltd
FPG International
Stock South

Commissioning Editor
Andrew Preston

Editorial
David Gibbon

Production
Ruth Arthur
Sally Connolly
Andrew Whitelaw

Director of Production
Gerald Hughes

CLB 2866
© 1992 Colour Library Books Ltd, Godalming, Surrey, England.
All rights reserved.
This 1992 edition published by Crescent Books,
distributed by Outlet Book Company, Inc., a Random House
Company, 40 Engelhard Avenue, Avenel, New Jersey 07001.
Printed and bound in Singapore.
ISBN 0 517 07275 0
8 7 6 5 4 3 2 1

FLORIDA
VACATIONLANDS
A PICTURE MEMORY

CRESCENT BOOKS
NEW YORK • AVENEL, NEW JERSEY

The people Floridians call "snowbirds" – the ones who swoop down on Florida at the first sign of flurries up north – are quite partisan about which part of the Sunshine State is best. Back home they debate the relative merits of the West Coast versus the East all summer long, but it's an argument nobody wins. After all, with 1,350 miles of coastline and nearly all of it gorgeous, who can say where's the best place in Florida to forget your troubles and soak up some rays?

Stephen Leatherman, that's who. As director of the University of Maryland's Laboratory for Coastal Research, Leatherman recently waded into the controversy by ranking all the beaches in the United States, purely in the interests of science, of course. He didn't carry a beach blanket and a giant can of sunblock from shore to shore, although he claims to have visited, or at least flown over, the lion's share of America's beachfront. But, for his survey, he mailed questionnaires to local experts and managers of 650 beaches in all parts of the country, asking them to report on such things as the softness and color of the sand, the quality of the surf and the amount of undertow. He queried them about average water and air temperatures and the number of sunny days, as well as cleanliness, crowding and crime. Number One on his list is on the Hawaiian Island of Maui, but the second and third are in Florida, as are no less than twenty-nine of the top fifty. Three of the five best are Florida beaches, in fact, but none of them is on either the West Coast or the East Coast. They are all in the northwest corner of the state, the part known as "the

Panhandle," also known as "the other Florida."

According to Leatherman, the best beach in Florida is right about dead center on the Emerald Coast, the State Recreation Area at Grayton Beach. "It's dynamite," says the professor. "There are waves, but they're not big and not dangerous. And the water is super clean." He might also have mentioned that the sand is super white and soft as a down comforter, that the Gulf is a soothing shade of blue-green, that the sky is the color of a sapphire, and that a walk along the beach leads to a nature trail through salt marshes where more than 250 species of birds, from ospreys to loons, go hunting and fishing.

Florida's Panhandle doesn't quite fit the usual image of a state filled with palm trees and orange groves. The vegetation there is more in the magnolia, live oak, Spanish moss tradition of the Deep South, and its towns are filled with Greek Revival and Queen Anne houses that fairly reek of Southern hospitality. Ironically though, the Old South seems to stop more than five hundred miles north of Key West. Except for the hospitality, that is. With more than thirty-seven million visitors a year, Floridians get plenty of practice at entertaining. And as proof that they're good at it, consider the number who decide to stay: back in 1950, the population was less than three million; today it is over twelve million and growing fast. Because if Florida is a great place to visit, it's also a terrific place to live.

One of the prevailing myths about the Sunshine State is that it is a mecca for retirees, and although there aren't many better places to retire, only about eighteen percent of Florida's population is over sixty-five, and exactly the same percentage is under fifteen. And if there is a generation gap, it doesn't show. It's a safe bet that every one of those kids has been or will soon be a guest in the house built in 1988 as a sixtieth birthday present for Florida's most popular citizen.

It's hard to think of Mickey Mouse as a senior citizen, even if the calendar says he's getting there, but in the lifetime of the parents who take their children to Walt Disney World, it would have seemed improbable that he'd ever move to Florida. Once the decision was made, in fact, it was one of the best-kept secrets in American history.

The snowbirds who argued among themselves over the relative merits of Florida's coasts had usually been silent about the inland scrub country. It was a land of dry sandhills filled with crawly creatures, as well as palmettos, pines and prickly pears. Cleared and irrigated, the Central Highlands were good for orange groves, and not bad for cattle ranching, but not of much interest to developers. It was why no one noticed when outsiders quietly began buying huge tracts of the land. Those who did notice were certain they were watching the biggest collection of fools that ever got suckered into the real estate game, and Florida had seen plenty of them. They all stopped laughing in 1965 when Walt Disney announced that he was planning an East Coast version of Disneyland, but by then it was too late for them to adjust their prices accordingly. Disney already owned 28,000 acres near Orlando, acquired at an average cost of $185 an acre. By the time the park opened six years later, an acre of once-worthless scrub land nearby was considered a steal at $300,000.

The values have been climbing ever since. Mickey Mouse's new house and the little community of Duckburg is the newest addition to Disney's original Magic Kingdom, but hardly a year has gone by since Walt Disney World was created that something new hasn't been added to improve the neighborhood. The original plan was not so much to build a carbon copy of Disneyland in California, but to improve on it. The first step was that clandestine assembling of real estate. When its gates opened in 1971, The Magic Kingdom itself covered just one hundred acres of a 2,500-acre development of lakes, golf courses and hotels. Most of the rest was left wild, as a buffer against the kind of sprawling development that usually comes with success. But

some was earmarked for expansion, too. Disney's dream was to complement his vacation center with a working community that would serve as a model for cities of the future. He called it the Experimental Prototype Community of Tomorrow – EPCOT for short. The dream died with him, but the name lived on, and Epcot Center, a 260-acre world's fair-like showcase of international lifestyle and gee-whiz futuristic technology, was created in 1982. Nobody lives there, as had been part of the original master plan, but about 25,000 work at Walt Disney World, including Mickey and Donald, and every one of them seems to be having just as much fun as the more than twenty-million visitors they entertain each year. In 1989, they were joined by Miss Piggy and Kermit the Frog and others at the Disney-MGM Studios Theme Park. The movie park covers one-hundred acres, and Typhoon Lagoon, where visitors can get away from it all by being shipwrecked on a tropical island, takes in another fifty, but Walt Disney World in Florida is still a place of open space. The undeveloped portion of the original tract is bigger than the Island of Manhattan with 10,000 acres to spare. Who knows what wonders will fill that space to delight your great-grandchildren?

The place to find out is probably at Cassadaga Spiritualist Camp north of Orlando, where mediums and psychics go for their winter vacations, but the fortune-tellers weren't too good at predicting Walt Disney World itself, even though along with everyone else they had a preview of it when Cypress Gardens opened near Winter Haven in 1936. It's the granddaddy of all the theme parks near Orlando, but more than 8,000 plants, from orchids and camellias to roses and water lilies keep it younger than springtime through every season. Back in the days when you got a newsreel along with your Saturday afternoon movie, water skiing shows featuring the Aquamaids on adjoining Lake Eloise were big news every couple of weeks, and even though the pictures were in black and white, thousands got the message and took off for Florida to see the real thing, making Cypress Gardens Florida's Number One attraction for a generation of Americans. And it's still high on the list in an area where the lures include, just for openers: Sea World and Universal Studios, Circus World and Gatorland, a Tupperware museum, a weekly livestock auction, wax museums, funhouses, golf courses and the Kennedy Space Center. All of which raises the inevitable question: is there anything going on in the rest of Florida? The answer is, of course: just name your pleasure.

For many visitors, the ultimate adventure is kicking off their shoes and using their toes to pick up shells on Sanibel Island near Fort Meyers, undisputed as the world's best beach for gathering such souvenirs. Others prefer to do their souvenir hunting along Worth Avenue in Palm Beach, where the baubles at Cartier's or Van Cleef & Arpels would never be mistaken for something washed up by the sea. For some, Miami is a perfect example of a tropical paradise with big-city conveniences and, if they feel a need for a little raw nature, they can always run over to the nearby Everglades and gape at some 'gators. Those who want to get away from it all get on the Overseas Highway for the spectacular 126-mile trip through the Florida Keys, where the temperature is cooler in summer and warmer in winter than anywhere else in the state, and the sunsets over the Gulf of Mexico magically take away the frustration of weekend traffic jams on the narrow highway. And if Florida's crowded roads, highrise beachfront resorts and futuristic parks make visitors long for a trip into the past, there is no town in America that can take them further back than St. Augustine, with its three-hundred year-old fort and a little village that was established in 1565. It is also the city that became Florida's first vacationland back in 1888, when Henry Flagler built two hotels there and called it the American Riviera.

It took Flagler twenty-four more years to extend his Florida East Coast Railroad all the way down to Key West, and on the way he put Palm Beach and Miami on the map. But if you were to ask the man who made his fortune with John D. Rockefeller's Standard Oil for his own choice of Florida's best vacationland, Palm Beach would surely be the place. It was just a sandbar when he first arrived there in 1893, but years earlier a shipload of coconuts had broken up in the surf and left a legacy of some 20,000 palm trees that seemed to be calling out for houses to shade. Flagler started the ball rolling by building the biggest wooden hotel the world has ever seen and carefully naming it, not for the coconut palms, but for another tree, the showy royal poinciana. As luck would have it, temperatures dropped to near the freezing mark there the following winter – something that has never happened again and is probably against the law in the Town of Palm Beach –and Flagler moved on to what appeared to be the more salubrious climate of Miami, where he set the wheels in motion to have it incorporated as a city and then built the Royal Palm Hotel as its centerpiece. But before moving any further south, he went back to Palm Beach and built a seventy-two-room mansion for his third wife, which became the trend setter for a community of similarly-opulent mansions where the super rich could gather for their annual season in the sun, which then, as now, extended from December 15 to February 22. Flagler also added a new hotel along the beach, which he called The Breakers. Its third incarnation, built by his widow in 1926, is one of the two or three most elegant hotels in the entire country.

The most magnificent houses in Palm Beach were designed by Addison Mizner, whose first commission after he arrived along with the Roaring Twenties was the Everglades Club, still a formidable symbol of the super-rich who pay $25,000 as an initiation fee and add $3,500 a year to stay in good standing during the ten-week season. But that's just the first cost. A Mizner house can cost as much as $10 million and, if it faces the ocean, fifty percent more. Obviously, it isn't possible to run such a house without servants, and in Palm Beach a maid and butler earn $75,000 a year between them, plus expenses, of course. They not only need to be fed, clothed and housed, but they also need a car for all the little errands they're expected to run. There is no point in living in an elegant house if it isn't used for entertaining, and the people who really count in Palm Beach stage dinner parties for thirty or more at least once a week. The average budget for them hovers around $7,500. In Palm Beach, however, budget isn't a word that is used very often.

But visitors watching their budgets aren't turned away at any of the three bridges that connect the island with the mainland. There is even a public beach there, although there is almost no public parking. But there are beaches in other places, and if a visitor wants to feel like a millionaire for a few hours, weekend matches at the Gulfstream Polo Club, the oldest of four in the area, are free. Even the greyhound races at the Palm Beach Kennel Club are available for only fifty cents admission.

When Addison Mizner ran out of prime locations for his Spanish-style mansions in Palm Beach, he invested his profits in thousands of acres of scrubby land just to the south, called it Boca Raton and made millions subdividing it into building lots. But he wasn't the first to make a killing in Florida real estate.

The excitement began after World War I, when former airmen who had been sent to Florida for training began to drift back. Their hosts knew an opportunity when they saw one, and before the boom ended with

7

a hurricane in 1926, seven billion dollars were invested in Florida land. It was the result of one of the biggest advertising blitzes of all time. Folks up north were promised free trips to the Sunshine State in return for a contract to own a piece of it. Big League baseball stars joined hands with bathing beauties and professional golfers to get the message across. Tin Pan Alley was grinding out such hits as *Moon Over Miami*, and Broadway stars were lured to local nightclubs, where it was hoped their glamour would rub off on the real estate agents.

One of the slickest of them wasn't even a Floridian and, like many of his fellow New Yorkers, he himself had originally been suckered into buying land sight-unseen. And the salesman was no less a person than Napoleon Bonaparte Broward, the Governor of the state. The price was good, just fifty cents an acre, but all of the half-million acres Richard J. Bolles bought was under water in the Everglades. They called it "over-flowed land" in those days. But Bowles rose to the occasion. He had already made millions selling water-starved farmland in Oregon, and although he had never been to Florida he was sure he could find enough prospective buyers who hadn't, either.

He began by marking off 180,000 acres on a map and then dividing it into 12,000 "farms," three quarters of which were less than ten acres. Then he dropped a town into the center, which was divided into 12,000 building lots on broad streets, with factories, churches and schools. The town, he said, would be known as "Progresso." The map was reprinted in a brochure that offered standard contracts good for one farm and one town site for $250 payable in convenient monthly instalments. The contracts weren't specific about which farms or which townsites a buyer would get. That would be decided once the majority of the 12,000

contracts were signed, at which time a board of trustees would make the appropriate assignments. The brochure didn't mention all that water, but did quote a government report that the land itself had never been touched by frost, and that it was rich enough to make fertilization a waste of time and money. And to back up the salesman's good faith, it also promised a reward of a thousand dollars plus expenses to anyone who could prove that the brochure's promises weren't true. It was a safe guarantee for Bolles. Most of his customers were farmers, government workers and teachers who could barely afford the ten-dollar monthly payments, let alone finance a trip to Florida to see what they were buying.

In defense of Mr. Bolles and Governor Broward, it should be mentioned that the state had started to drain the Everglades and reclaim the land, and that the speculator himself was donating two dollars an acre to help do the job. But by 1911, the project was bogged down in politics and the land Bolles was selling was still over-flowed. Meanwhile, a Missouri Congressman recently returned from a junket to Miami called for an investigation into what he called "one of the meanest swindles ever devised or conducted anywhere in the country." The victims of the scheme had already begun to smell a rat and tried to take Bolles to court, but when they found that the legal fees would be higher than the $250 they had already invested, they decided to cut their losses. The Post Office finally took on the case and sued Bolles for fraudulent use of the mails. But to stand trail, he needed to be extradited to Kansas City where his company was chartered, and the seventy-four year-old Bolles cheated the hangman, so to speak, by dropping dead aboard his private railroad car just as it was pulling out of Palm Beach.

St. Mark's National Wildlife Refuge (facing page), in Apalachicola National Forest, is heaven on earth for bird-watchers and nature lovers.

Below: a sandy path leads to the lighthouse at St. Mark's National Wildlife Refuge. It is not hard to see why the Panhandle coastline from Pensacola to Panama City is known as the Miracle Strip (remaining pictures). Here miles of white sand border crystal-clear water, tempting even the most stalwart of landlubbers. East Pass (center right), a strip of water separating Destin from Fort Walton Beach, links Choctawhatchee Bay (top right) and the Gulf of Mexico. Overleaf: Holiday Island.

Jacksonville (these pages), center of Florida's industry and shipping, has the reputation of being "the working son in the Florida family of playboys." The city, which has grown up on both sides of St. Johns River, is the largest in the U.S. in terms of the land area that it covers. The Independent Life Insurance Company Building (top right), at thirty-seven stories the tallest building in the State, dominates the city's skyline. Annually, rival fans cram into Jacksonville's Gator Bowl (below) to watch the Georgia-Florida football game. Overleaf: Ponte Vedra Beach, one of the magnificent Atlantic Ocean beaches near Jacksonville.

18

St. Augustine (these pages) is the oldest continuously inhabited settlement in the continental U.S. The Ponce de Leon in St. Augustine (above, top right and below), one of the magnificent hotels built by railroad magnate Henry Flagler, now houses Flagler College. At Castillo de San Marcos (facing page), the largest as well as the oldest building in the city, costumed volunteers help recreate some of the atmosphere of the ancient Spanish fort. Bottom right: County Court House.

The expanse of compacted sand at Daytona Beach (these pages) provided an ideal surface for testing automobiles, and in the 1920s and '30s the beach was a renowned speedway. Modern-day Daytona Beach is fast becoming the number one spot for college students during the Spring Break and the only automobiles traveling on the beach do so at a sedate ten miles an hour. Overleaf: the John F. Kennedy Space Center.

Orlando (these pages), surrounded by theme parks, has become something of a tourist mecca. The face of the once-sleepy city is now characterized by sophisticated high-rises and hotels. Spaceship Earth (below) stands at the entrance to the EPCOT Center. A new word, "geosphere," was coined to describe properly the building which was like no pre-existing structure.

The site for Walt Disney World Vacation Kingdom (these pages) was chosen in 1963. Walt Disney died before his dream became reality, but the Kingdom, which can claim to be the world's most popular tourist attraction, must have surpassed his greatest expectations. Below: Cinderella Castle, the centerpiece of the Magic Kingdom, situated at the end of Main Street U.S.A.

Over sixty years after he was created, Micky Mouse (right) is still the uncrowned king of Disney characters. A massive floral tribute outside Main Street Railroad Station (facing page), at the gateway to the Magic Kingdom, is proof of his enduring popularity. Other favorites, including Goofey (above), Dopey (top right), Pooh Bear (below) and Uncle Remus' Brer Fox (bottom right) are also brought to life and young admirers can meet with their larger-than-life friends.

Trains on the Monorail (facing page top), which has been nicknamed the "highway in the sky," swish past Spaceship Earth transporting visitors to and from the EPCOT Center. The EPCOT Center's World Showcase recreates aspects of some of the world's different cultures. Inside the reconstruction of Peking's Temple of Heaven (below and facing page bottom) a CircleVision 360 film is shown giving an insight into life in modern China.

At Sea World (right) water skiing takes on a new meaning. For those with sense of adventure Busch Gardens offers a ride down a simulated Congo River (below). Roller coasters at Busch Gardens (top right) and Circus World (above) offer excitement for those with strong stomachs. Cypress Gardens (facing page) offers more tranquil pastimes.

The high-rises of downtown Tampa (top left) dominate the city skyline. St. Petersburg is a sailing center of repute whose prestigious racing events draw world class yachts. St. Petersburg Beach (bottom left), an island connected to the mainland by bridges, boasts hotels like the elegant, long-established Don Cesar (center left) at Pass-a-Grille. Below: aptly named Clearwater Beach offers superb watersports. Overleaf: Tarpon Springs, first of the fashionable Gulf Coast resorts.

Known as the Suncoast, Florida's southwestern coastline (top left and center left) has sun, sand, and surf in abundance. Beautiful scenery, miles of pure white sand, and fine fishing has made Marco Island (bottom left) a particular favorite with tourists in recent years. Below: Sarasota skyline seen from the boat harbor. Overleaf: C'ad'zan, home of John Ringling, the famous circus master.

Facing page top: aerial view of Goodyear blimp over Pompano Beach. Below: a cluster of palms give Hollywood Beach a desert island ambience. Palm Beach (remaining pictures) is a haven for the super rich and the resort is the center of the winter social scene. The exclusive Breakers Hotel (top left), built by Henry Flagler, and the Biltmore Hotel (left) epitomize the genteel elegance of the resort. Flagler's own Palm Beach mansion (bottom left) has been turned into a museum.

It took a lot of persuading to get railroad tycoon Henry Flagler to extend the line as far as Miami (these pages). This achieved, the city grew rapidly though erratically. Heat and humidity make sailing and watersports popular with Miami's well-heeled. Boats cram into the city's marinas (below) and a variety of working and pleasure craft can be seen on its waterways (facing page bottom). Renaissance-style Villa Vizcaya (left), with its ornate gardens, was built by industrialist James Deering. Miami Beach (overleaf), Miami's sister city, was once among Florida's top resorts. Though recent years have seen a decline in tourism, the resort is still popular with winter vacationers.

Miami is home to a host of wildlife parks. Miami's Metrozoo (top left) is home to rare species like the white tiger. Exotic pink flamingos stalk around Flamingo Lake (bottom left) at Parrot Jungle. At Seaquarium (below), a vast complex situated beside Biscayne Bay, audiences watch trainers put killer whales and dolphins through their paces. Center left: Fairchild Tropical Garden, complete with a simulated rain forest.

The unique, natural beauty of southern Florida has been preserved in Everglades National Park (these pages). Its dense tangles of cypress trees (below) and open expanses of saw-grass are home to many species mammals and birds, as well as the famous gators. Parts of the wide, shallow river (facing page bottom), dubbed by the Indians the "river of grass," are patrolled by park wardens on airboats. Facing page top: great egrets and a wood stork feeding on water lettuce.

The Florida Keys (these pages) – the name derives from a corruption of the Spanish word "cayo," meaning "little island" – are a string of islands stretching out from Biscayne Bay for 180 miles. Protected by a coral reef, the inner waters of the Keys provide good sailing and fishing all year round. Overleaf: the original Seven Mile Bridge, an engineering marvel, bends only once, at Pigeon Key.

A huge mural welcoming visitors Key Largo (top right) celebrates its superb marine life. At Southernmost Point (above), Key West is nearer Cuba than mainland America. A patriotic show of flags in Key West's Front Street (facing page top), however, firmly declares its allegiance. The Conch Train (center right) tours the Old Town, which is still rich with character. Sponges, once an important factor in Key West's economy, are sold along with conch shells in numerous local markets (remaining pictures). Overleaf: lighthouse on Marathon Key.

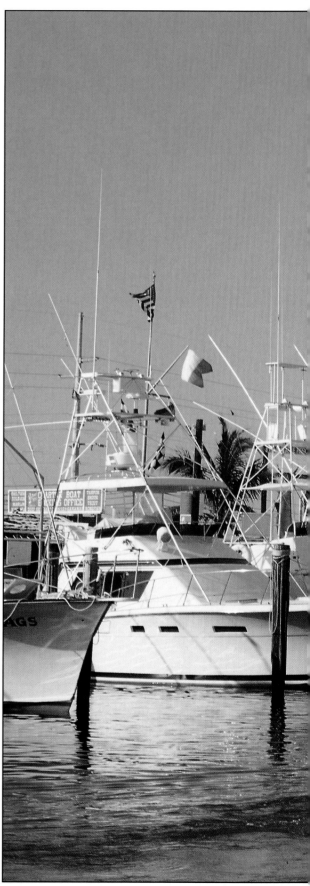

On Upper Matecumbe Key (these pages) sport fishing is big business. A whole fleet of boats are available for hire, and vacationers can take off with rod and reel to try their luck. Though old-timers swear that the fish are neither as big nor as numerous as they were in the past, catches are still impressive. Overleaf: a solitary boat makes its way across Whale Harbor. Following page: Bahia Honda State Park.